Amending the Constitution

by Eric Oatman

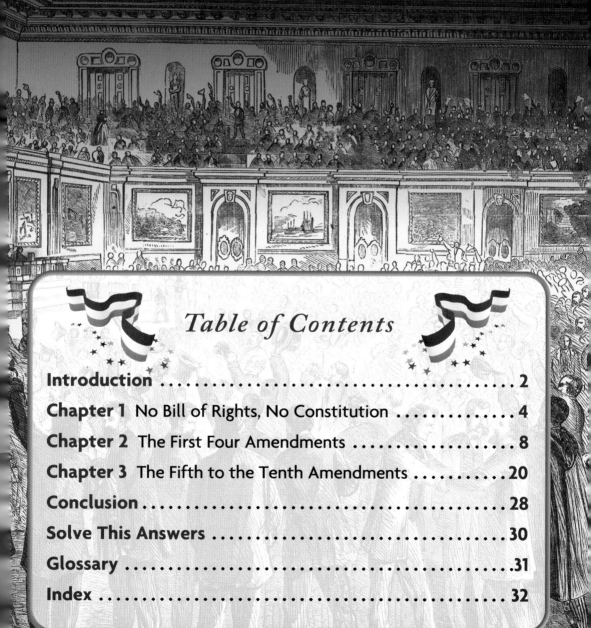

Table of Contents

Introduction

In 1734, New York was not yet a state. It was one of Great Britain's thirteen colonies in America. The colony of New York was ruled by a dishonest man named William Cosby. A printer for a newspaper called the *New-York Weekly Journal* wrote about Cosby's misdeeds. The printer's name was John Peter Zenger.

William Cosby got mad. He put the printer in jail. Then he charged Zenger with **libel**, or lying about someone in print. Cosby made Zenger suffer.

Zenger had to wait eight months for his trial to start. His **bail** was set so high he couldn't pay it. He had to stay in jail the whole time.

During the trial, Zenger's lawyer argued that it was not a crime to publish things that were true. He said, "It is . . . a right, which all free men claim, that they are entitled to complain when they are hurt." A jury agreed. Zenger went free.

Fifty-seven years later, the right that Zenger's lawyer spoke about—and several other rights—became part of the United States Constitution. Americans decided to **amend**, or change, the Constitution by adding ten important sentences. Together, the ten sentences are called the Bill of Rights. This book will explain what freedoms the Bill of Rights protects and how the Constitution can be amended.

The United States in 1790

New Hampshire
Maine (part of Massachusetts)
Massachusetts
Lake Huron
Lake Ontario
New York
Lake Erie
Rhode Island
Connecticut
Pennsylvania
New Jersey
Delaware
Virginia
Maryland
North Carolina
Atlantic Ocean
South Carolina
Georgia
Gulf of Mexico

N
W E
S

About four million people lived in the United States in 1790. ▲ Most people lived in the original thirteen states. The rest made their homes in Vermont, Kentucky, Tennessee, and Maine. These would become states between 1791 and 1820.

No Bill of Rights, No Constitution

On September 17, 1787, most of the men who wrote the U.S. Constitution gathered to sign it. They had created a six-page plan for a new form of government. The plan described the duties of three branches of government.

The executive branch would carry out laws. The legislative branch would pass laws. The judicial branch would form a system of national courts.

The plan was brilliant. However, at least three of the Framers, the men who wrote the Constitution, felt it wasn't complete. They wanted the Constitution to contain a bill of rights, or list of freedoms. George Mason said, "I would sooner chop off my right hand than put it to the Constitution as it now stands."

▼ Most of the states that voted for the Constitution wanted a bill of rights added.

Most of the delegates were tired. They wanted the Constitution to be signed. Therefore, thirty-eight of the delegates, including George Washington, signed the document. The three delegates who wanted a bill of rights did not.

People in the thirteen states then had to **ratify**, or approve, the Constitution. Many people voted against the Constitution because it did not have a bill of rights. In the end, the Constitution was approved, but it was clear that a bill of rights was needed.

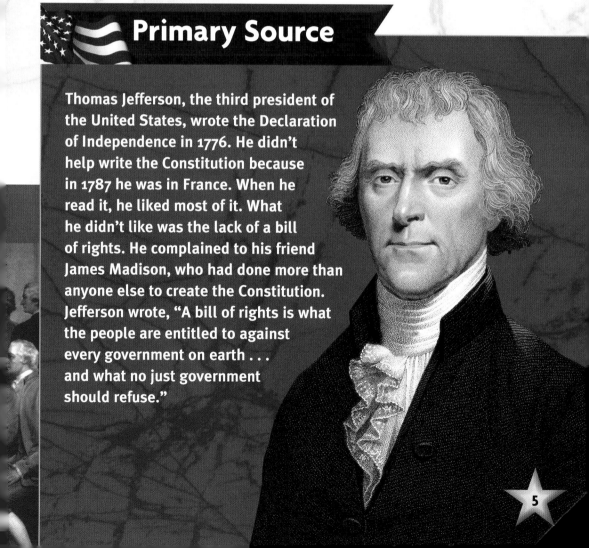

Primary Source

Thomas Jefferson, the third president of the United States, wrote the Declaration of Independence in 1776. He didn't help write the Constitution because in 1787 he was in France. When he read it, he liked most of it. What he didn't like was the lack of a bill of rights. He complained to his friend James Madison, who had done more than anyone else to create the Constitution. Jefferson wrote, "A bill of rights is what the people are entitled to against every government on earth . . . and what no just government should refuse."

Federalists and Anti-Federalists

The fight over a bill of rights went public as soon as newspapers published the Constitution. People who were in favor of the Constitution without a bill of rights called themselves Federalists. They wanted a **federal system**, a type of government in which power is shared by national and state governments.

The people against the Constitution were called Anti-Federalists. They liked the idea of a federal system, but they thought the Constitution made the states too weak. They were also concerned that the national government might be powerful enough to take away the rights of the states.

The Ratification of the Constitution

State	Date each state ratified the Constitution	Delegates' yes votes	Delegates' no votes	Percentage of voters who said yes
1. Delaware	Dec. 7, 1787	30	0	100%
2. Pennsylvania	Dec. 12, 1787	46	23	67%
3. New Jersey	Dec. 18, 1787	38	0	
4. Georgia	Jan. 2, 1788	26	0	100%
5. Connecticut	Jan. 9, 1788	128	40	
6. Massachusetts	Feb. 6, 1788	187	168	53%
7. Maryland	April 28, 1788	63	11	85%
8. South Carolina	May 23, 1788	149	73	67%
9. New Hampshire	June 21, 1788	57	47	
10. Virginia	June 25, 1788	89	79	53%
11. New York	July 26, 1788	30	27	
12. North Carolina	Nov. 21, 1789	194	77	72%
13. Rhode Island	May 29, 1790	34	32	52%

To win the votes of Anti-Federalists, the Federalists made a promise. If the states ratified the Constitution, the Federalists would work hard to get it amended. They would make sure the Constitution contained a list of rights that no government could take away.

The promise satisfied many Anti-Federalists. The states ratified the Constitution. The nation's first president, George Washington, took office on April 30, 1789. Two months later, Congressman James Madison presented seventeen Constitutional amendments to the U.S. Congress.

THE

FEDERALIST:

A COLLECTION

OF

ESSAYS,

WRITTEN IN FAVOUR OF THE

NEW CONSTITUTION,

AS AGREED UPON BY THE FEDERAL CONVENTION,
SEPTEMBER 17, 1787.

IN TWO VOLUMES.

VOL. I.

NEW-YORK:

PRINTED AND SOLD BY J. AND A. McLEAN,
No. 41, HANOVER-SQUARE.
M.DCC.LXXXVIII.

★ Solve This

The table on page 6 shows the percentage of yes votes in nine states. What was the percentage of yes votes in the remaining four?

MATH ✔ POINT

How could you check your work?

◀ The Federalists published papers that explained their position. People can see those papers today in Washington, D.C.

The First Four Amendments

Congress was not eager to decide on Madison's proposed amendments. They wanted to wait. But Madison wouldn't give up. Finally, Congress reviewed the amendments.

The Constitution requires the approval of two-thirds of the members of the House of Representatives and the Senate to pass an amendment. Both houses of Congress passed twelve amendments in late September. Then they sent the amendments to the states for ratification.

The states voted down two amendments that did not deal with personal freedoms. Those amendments dealt with pay for members of Congress, and the number of people each member would represent. The states took two years to pass the ten amendments that became the Bill of Rights.

Eleven states had to approve the Bill of Rights before it became law. In 1791, Virginia became the eleventh state to ratify the Bill of Rights.

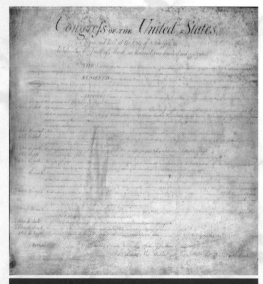

▲ **The Bill of Rights was passed on December 15, 1791.**

Two Ways to Amend the Constitution

The Framers provided two ways to amend the Constitution. One way lets the U.S. Congress propose an amendment. The other way lets the states propose an amendment. Here's how each method works.

When the U.S. Congress wants to amend the Constitution

Step 1 Two-thirds of the members of each house of Congress must pass an amendment before the proposal can be sent to the states for ratification.

Step 2 The legislatures, or law-making bodies, in three-fourths of the states must ratify the amendment.

When the states want to amend the Constitution

Step 1 The legislatures in two-thirds of the states must agree on the need for an amendment. Then those states ask Congress to set up a national convention to propose the amendment.

Step 2 The legislators, or delegates to the conventions from three-fourths of the states, must ratify the amendment.

The First Amendment, Part 1: Freedom of Religion

"Congress shall make no law respecting an establishment of religion, or prohibiting the free exercise thereof . . ."

In the early 1600s, the king of England allowed Christians to belong to only one type of church, the Church of England. A group of people called Puritans thought the Church of England was too fancy. They tried to worship in a simpler way. The king punished them. So, in 1620, a group of Puritans fled to America and established a colony. But the Puritans acted like the king they left behind. They wanted everyone in the colony to worship one way.

The Ratification of the Bill of Rights

State	Date
1. New Jersey	Nov. 20, 1789
2. Maryland	Dec. 19, 1789
3. North Carolina	Dec. 22, 1789
4. South Carolina	Jan. 19, 1790
5. New Hampshire	Jan. 25, 1790
6. Delaware	Jan. 28, 1790
7. New York	Feb. 24, 1790
8. Pennsylvania	Mar. 10, 1790
9. Rhode Island	June 7, 1790
10. Vermont	Nov. 3, 1791
11. Virginia	Dec. 15, 1791
12. Massachusetts	Mar. 2, 1939
13. Georgia	Mar. 18, 1939
14. Connecticut	Apr. 19, 1939

When Virginia adopted the Bill of Rights, it became law.

2 Solve This

How much time passed between the year Virginia ratified the Bill of Rights and the year the final three states ratified the Bill of Rights?

MATH ✔ POINT

How could you check your work?

This upset Anne Hutchinson. She began to preach to a small group of women in her house. The leaders of the colony heard about it. They put Hutchinson on trial for trying to overthrow the government. Then, they made her leave the colony.

The Framers were thinking of cases like Anne Hutchinson's when they wrote the First Amendment. The government set up by the Puritans allowed for only one way to worship. The First Amendment made sure that could not happen again. In the words of Thomas Jefferson, the First Amendment builds "a wall of separation between church and state."

Anne Hutchinson left Massachusetts and went to Rhode Island. She was described as "a woman of active spirit . . . more bold than a man."

✔ **POINT**

Picture It

Draw a picture of Anne Hutchinson inviting some women from the colony to a meeting at her home. Use speech balloons to show what each person is saying.

The First Amendment, Part 2: Freedom of Expression

*"Congress shall make no law…abridging the freedom of speech, or of the press; or the right of the people peaceably to assemble, and to **petition** the Government for a redress of grievances."*

The right for people to question their government is an important freedom.

Freedom of speech and of the press means that many different ideas may be written, said, and read by the people. Before the Bill of Rights, those freedoms were sometimes barred. In 1788, a Philadelphia printer questioned the fairness of a judge. He was jailed and fined. That same year, a Massachusetts court fined a judge. He wrote that citizens should "disturb the government" if the government would not listen to their complaints.

▲ Eleazar Oswald, a Philadelphia printer, spent a month in jail for saying that a judge was unfair.

The judge wasn't promoting free speech. He was arguing for the right of Americans to petition, or ask, the government to listen to them. The First Amendment gives all Americans the right to expect their government to deal with their complaints.

Americans also have the right to march or hold rallies to call attention to their complaints. The gatherings must be peaceful, though. In 1965, the U.S. Supreme Court said that without "public order, liberty itself would be lost."

▲ Dr. Martin Luther King, Jr. exercised his right to march peacefully when he marched for equal rights.

Careers

Journalist

John Peter Zenger was a printer, one of two in New York City in the 1700s. But he became a journalist when he started his newspaper. Today, most journalists are reporters. Some gather news and write about it for newspapers and magazines. Others record the news on video or audiotape for TV and radio stations.

▲ Journalists often interview people while covering a story.

The Second Amendment: The Right to Bear Arms

*"A well-regulated **militia**, being necessary to the security of a free State, the right of the people to keep and bear Arms, shall not be infringed."*

A distant bell woke up Sylvanus Wood before dawn on April 19, 1775. He knew that the bell meant trouble. He ran out the door with his gun. At that time, most people owned guns that they used for hunting and for protection.

Sylvanus was a member of a militia, or a group of ordinary citizens who were expected to defend their town at a moment's notice. Sylvanus lived in the town of Lexington, Massachusetts. He joined the other militiamen. About 900 British soldiers entered Lexington. The soldiers were headed to Concord. Their goal was to capture and destroy the militia's guns.

Eyewitness Account

A Militia Meets the Redcoats
Sylvanus Wood described what he saw in Lexington:

"The British troops approached rapidly in platoons, with a general officer on horseback at their head. . . . The officer swung his sword and said, 'Lay down your arms, or you are all dead men. . . .' Captain Parker [the militia company's leader] ordered every man take care of himself . . . [Then] the British fired and killed some of our men."

The Framers wrote the Second Amendment to prevent the U.S. government from taking guns away from its citizens. Some say the Framers also meant to give people who were not in militias the right to own guns. In 2001, a court in New Orleans agreed. But in 2002, a court in San Francisco disagreed.

The Massachusetts militiamen did not give up their guns. They chased the British all the way back to Boston.

3 Solve This

Experts say that U.S. citizens own 30 times more firearms than Canadians. Canadians are estimated to own 7.4 million firearms. If this number is correct, about how many firearms are in private hands in the United States?

MATH ✔ POINT

Is your answer reasonable? Why or why not?

▼ The Battle of Lexington and Concord showed the need for the Second Amendment.

15

The Third Amendment: Protection from Quartering Troops

*"No Soldier shall, in time of peace, be **quartered** in any house without the consent of the Owner . . ."*

In 1765, the British passed a law called the Quartering Act. The law forced American colonists to quarter, or house, British soldiers in inns and stables. Americans had to feed them, too—all for free.

The Quartering Act was hard on the citizens of cities like Boston and New York City. Boston was a city of about 16,000 people. The people there had to find room for about 5,000 British troops. New York City had to house thousands more. The British army had its headquarters in New York City.

In 1774, the British passed a tougher Quartering Act. Now the colonists had to let soldiers live with them in their homes.

The Third Amendment protects a homeowner's right to refuse to quarter soldiers. The only possible exception is during wartime, if Congress requires it.

The Third Amendment tells us that the colonists valued their privacy, just as families do today. It also reminds us of the harsh British laws that caused Americans to fight for their freedom.

▲ It was a hardship for colonists to feed and house the British soldiers.

⭐4 Solve This

The Quartering Acts required colonists to house British soldiers in barns, inns, and even private homes. Suppose a building could hold five soldiers. About how many buildings would be needed to quarter all the soldiers in Boston?

MATH ✔ POINT

How could you check your work?

The Fourth Amendment: Protection from Search and Seizure

"The right of the people to be secure in their persons, houses, papers, and effects, against unreasonable searches and seizures, shall not be violated, and no **Warrants** *shall issue but upon probable cause. . . ."*

The Fourth Amendment protects a person's right to privacy. Why did the Framers write this law? The colonists had to pay **duties**, or import taxes, on goods. Some people did not want to pay. So they turned to smuggling. They found ways to sneak imports like glass, lead, paints, and tea past tax collectors.

Historical Perspective

When they wrote the Fourth Amendment, the Framers weren't thinking about wiretapping. Today, law enforcement officers can search for and seize evidence by listening to private conversations, but they must have a warrant to do so. To get one, they must prove to a judge that the person they want to listen to may have committed or is committing a crime.

The tax collectors fought back. They barged into colonists' homes and shops to search for smuggled goods whenever and wherever they wanted. The tax collectors could do that because they carried writs of assistance. A writ of assistance was a type of warrant. The writs gave permission from a judge to search and seize evidence of a crime. Tax collectors, soldiers, and sheriffs could get warrants easily. They didn't have to say who or where they wanted to search, or even give a reason for the search.

Primary Source

The colonists hated the power the writs gave to British officials. In 1772, a man in Boston said:

"Our houses and even our bed chambers, are exposed to be ransacked, our boxes, chests and trunks broke open . . . and plundered by wretches." The "wretches" were the hated tax collectors.

This hand-colored woodcut ▶ shows a blacksmith being served a writ of assistance.

The Fifth to the Tenth Amendments

The Fifth Amendment: The Right to Fair Treatment

"No person shall be held to answer for a capital, or otherwise infamous crime, unless on a presentment or indictment of a Grand Jury . . . Nor shall any person be subject for the same offense to be twice put in jeopardy of life or limb . . . nor be deprived of life, liberty, or property, without due process of law. . . ."

Before 1776, the king of England ruled the American colonies. Colonists had many of the same rights that people in England did. The Framers wanted their new government to respect those rights.

So they wrote the Fifth Amendment. It requires the government to:

- Let a grand jury, a panel of citizens, decide if the government has enough evidence to try someone accused of a crime;
- Ban **double jeopardy**, or trying someone twice for the same crime;
- Allow accused persons to choose not to testify at their own trials;
- Give people a fair and reasonable opportunity to defend themselves;
- Pay property owners fairly for land needed for public use, such as for roads and dams.

Juries often decide whether a person is guilty or innocent.

The Sixth Amendment: The Right to a Fair Trial

". . . the accused shall enjoy the right to a speedy and public trial . . . to be confronted with the witnesses against him . . . and to have the Assistance of Counsel for his defense."

The Sixth Amendment also protects the rights of people accused of crimes. It requires the government to:

- Give a person accused of a crime a speedy and public trial;
- Use a jury to decide whether an accused person is guilty or innocent;
- Tell an accused person what he is being charged with and why;
- Let an accused person come face-to-face with his accuser;
- Let an accused person call people who may help her case to testify in court;
- Provide a lawyer for a person accused of committing a crime.

It's a Fact

Women were not allowed to serve on juries until 1920 when they won the right to vote.

The Seventh Amendment: Rights in Civil Cases

"In suits at common law . . . the right of trial by jury shall be preserved and no fact . . . shall be otherwise reexamined in any Court of the United States, than according to the rules of the common law."

Courts try people accused of committing crimes, but they also settle disputes between people or groups. If an adult stole your bike, the case would end up in criminal court. If your bike was crushed by a speeding car, your parents might sue the driver. That case would end up in civil court.

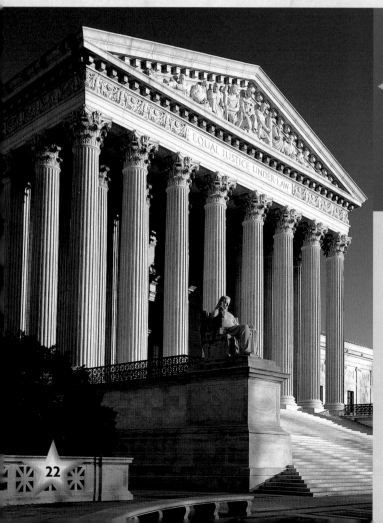

◄ The Supreme Court is the highest court in the United States. It is the final court of appeal.

✔ POINT

Reread

Reread the direct quotes in the Primary Source and Eyewitness Account sidebars. Why do you think the author included these in the book?

The Seventh Amendment states that juries should decide cases in civil courts. If a person doesn't like the jury's decision, he can ask a higher court to take another look. But the higher court must make a decision based only on the evidence presented to the lower court.

They Made a Difference

▼ Madison is often called the "Father of the Constitution."

No one did more to shape the U.S. Constitution and the Bill of Rights than James Madison. He was born into a very rich family in Virginia in 1751. He was a sickly child. He never weighed more than 100 pounds (45 kilograms), even as an adult. Yet when it came to building a new government, Madison was one of the nation's most powerful men.

Madison played a leading role at the 1787 Constitutional Convention in Philadelphia. He wrote the Bill of Rights in 1789. He pushed the first Congress to pass it. In 1809, he became the nation's fourth president. When he died in 1836, he was one of the country's most popular leaders. He also had a good sense of humor. He said, "If men were angels, no government would be necessary."

23

The Eighth Amendment: Restraints on Punishment

"Excessive bail shall not be required, nor excessive fines imposed, nor cruel and unusual punishments inflicted."

The Eighth Amendment reminds the government that it cannot do these three things:

- Set bail so high that a person accused of a crime is unable to pay it;

- Punish a person with a fine that is much larger than what others have paid for committing the same crime;

- Punish a person in a cruel way, or in a way that isn't commonly used.

In My Opinion

Some people think that the death penalty is a cruel punishment. Others think it is fair for certain crimes. Some states allow the death penalty, while others do not.

Some states still use the ▶ electric chair to carry out the death penalty in some murder cases.

Earlier you read about what happened to John Peter Zenger in 1734. People accused of crimes can stay out of jail while waiting for their trials. To do that, they must leave some money with the court. That money is called bail.

If the accused person returns for his trial, he gets his bail money back. If he doesn't return, he loses it.

The Eighth Amendment says that it is illegal to set bail so high that an accused person cannot afford it. It is also illegal to make a guilty person pay a $10,000 fine when others guilty of the same offense have paid only $1,000.

At what point does punishment become cruel? People have different views on that subject.

Historical Perspective

Until 1641, a British court called the Star Chamber held sessions in secret. There were no juries, no witnesses, and no clear charges. The court was used to try rebels, including Puritans like those who fled to New England. Today, that would be illegal, thanks to the Bill of Rights.

The Ninth Amendment: Rights Not Listed

"The enumeration in the Constitution of certain rights shall not be construed to deny or disparage others retained by the people."

Some people didn't want a bill of rights. In fact, they thought a bill of rights could be dangerous. That's because any enumeration, or list, would always be incomplete. A government might decide not to respect certain rights unless they were on a list.

Madison solved the problem with the twenty-one well-chosen words of the Ninth Amendment. He made sure that people would be able to enjoy freedoms that were not specifically listed in the Bill of Rights, as well as the freedoms that were listed.

▲ Today, people campaign for amendments to the Constitution for rights not listed.

The Tenth Amendment: Powers Not Given

"The powers not delegated to the United States by the Constitution, nor prohibited by it to the states, are reserved to the states respectively, or to the people."

The Tenth Amendment, like the Ninth, limits the power of the federal government. When the Constitution was written, each state saw itself as a separate country. No state wanted to turn all its powers over to a central government.

The Tenth Amendment addresses that issue. The Constitution gives the national government several powers. The national government may declare war, print money, and make treaties. State governments have several powers, too. States may issue licenses, ratify amendments, set up local governments, and act to protect the public health. According to the Tenth Amendment, the states' list of powers can grow longer. The states, or the American people, are granted any powers that the Constitution does not give to the national government.

5 Solve This

New Hampshire became the last state needed to ratify the Constitution in June of 1788. In December of 1791, Virginia became the last state needed to ratify the Bill of Rights. How many months passed between the ratification of the Constitution and the ratification of the Bill of Rights?

MATH ✔ POINT

What steps did you follow to get your answer?

▲ Each state legislature works to pass laws to protect and to help the residents of its state.

Conclusion

The Bill of Rights is a special document. It protects a person's right to criticize the government. It allows people to worship as they please. It protects people from searches and seizures that are not reasonable. It also gives people the right to defend their lives, liberties, and property.

The states have ratified seventeen amendments in addition to the first ten that make up the Bill of Rights.

When All 27 Amendments Became Laws

1 to 10
Bill of Rights, 1791

1790 1800 1810 1820 1830 1840 1850 1860 1870 1880 1890 1900 1910 1920 1930 1940

11
1795

13
1865

16 & 17
1913

20 & 21
1933

12
1804

14
1868

18
1919

15
1870

19
1920

The Twenty-Seventh Amendment was ratified in 1992. It deals with the pay that the members of the U.S. House of Representatives and Senate receive for serving in Congress.

The Bill of Rights is only 462 words. Those words were written more than 200 years ago, but they are as important today as they were in 1791. They define the freedoms that all Americans enjoy.

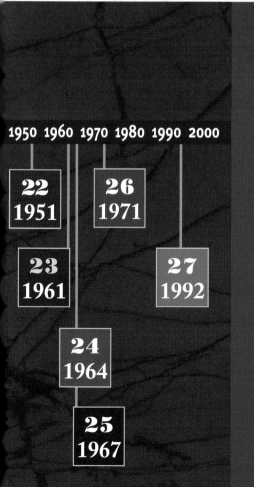

1950 1960 1970 1980 1990 2000

22 1951

26 1971

23 1961

27 1992

24 1964

25 1967

Here is a list of amendments that experts identify as several of the most important.

- The first ten amendments spell out many key rights.

- The 13th ended slavery.

- The 14th guarantees rights and privileges to United States citizens.

- The 15th bars the federal and state governments from keeping citizens from voting because of their race, color, or the fact that they were once enslaved.

- The 19th prohibits the federal and state governments from keeping women from voting.

- The 26th grants the right to vote to anyone eighteen years old and above.

Solve This Answers

1. **Page 7**
   New Jersey: 100%
   Connecticut: 128 + 40 = 168 total delegates
   128/168 = .761 or 76%
   New Hampshire: 57 + 47 = 104 total delegates
   57/104 = .548 or 55%
   New York: 30 + 27 = 57 total delegates
   30/57 = .526 or 53%

2. **Page 10**
   Virginia ratified the Bill of Rights in 1791.
   The final three states ratified it in 1939.
   1939 − 1791 = 148 years

3. **Page 15**
   7.4 X 30 = 222
   If the estimates are correct, there are about 222 million firearms
   in private hands in the United States.

4. **Page 17**
   5,000/5 = 1,000
   If each building held 5 soldiers, about 1,000 buildings would
   be needed to quarter 5,000 troops.

5. **Page 27**
   The Constitution was ratified in June of 1788. The Bill of Rights
   was ratified in December of 1791.
   June 1788 to June 1791 = 3 years, or 36 months
   June 1791 to December 1791 = 6 months
   36 + 6 = 42
   42 months passed between the ratification dates of the two documents.

Glossary

amend — (uh-MEND) to change formally, according to an official procedure (page 3)

bail — (BALE) money given to a court of law to allow an arrested person to remain out of jail until trial (page 2)

double jeopardy — (DUH-bul JEH-per-dee) protection against being put on trial twice for the same offense (page 20)

duty — (DOO-tee) a tax paid on goods that are brought into or taken out of a country (page 18)

federal system — (FEH-duh-rul SIS-tem) a type of government in which the national and state governments share power (page 6)

libel — (LY-bul) to lie about someone in print (page 2)

militia — (mih-LIH-shuh) an army of ordinary citizens that is used in emergencies (page 14)

petition — (peh-TIH-shun) a formal request that is made to a person in authority (page 12)

quarter — (KWOR-ter) to house (page 16)

ratify — (RA-tih-fy) to agree to officially; to approve (page 5)

warrant — (WOR-unt) a judge's written permission to search for and seize evidence of a crime (page 18)

Index